And Then There Was Hope

by:

Angie Odom

with

Abby Morris-Frye

All profits the authors receive from the sale of this book will be given to Hope and the TLC Community Center in Elizabethton, TN.

Copyright © 2014 Angie Odom and Journey of Hope Outreach. Published in the United States of America. All rights reserved. No part of this book may be reproduced in any form or by any electronic or mechanical means, including information storage and retrieval systems, without permission in writing by the author. Your support of the author's rights is appreciated.

This book tells the story of a little girl named Hope Odom. While the events of this story are true, the names of some individuals were changed to protect their identity or privacy.

This book is dedicated to my

daughter Hope.

I pray you will always see the

miracle from God you truly are

and share the love of God everywhere

you go, giving hope to others.

Forward

Just when you think you have your life in order and your children are grown, God sends you on a new adventure. This is where my husband and I found ourselves in 2013 – on an adventure, with God leading the way. We now have a new understanding of the meanings of the phrases "let go and let God", "put your trust in God", and "miracles do happen."

This book is one of those things that God woke me up early and put a burden on my heart to start writing. As I prayed in bed talking to God I was giving Him every reason why I couldn't and shouldn't start writing. But God stopped me in my tracks and said to me "There's Hope." My mind started reflecting on the last 18 months and how hope was shown around every corner, even when things seemed grim.

My prayer in writing this book and sharing the story of Hope is every person can hear that miracles still happen. That no matter where you are or what you are doing in life, God can blow you out of the water when you least expect it. I also pray that people will be inspired to reach out to others with more of an unconditional love than ever before, choosing to love others - wanting nothing in return - even when that person doesn't deserve it. It is written to share the truth of about consequences of choices made with the understanding of how God never leaves us or forsakes us. It has taught me that no matter what we are facing God has it under control, if we will just give up trying to control the situation ourselves.

No matter what you do in life - EMS, fireman, police, nurse, pastor, garbage man, dispatcher, stay-at-home mom - God has a purpose for your life. You never know what moment He may use YOU in HIS miracle.

I pray people will come to accept Christ in their hearts and lives with a better understanding that without Him there is no Hope. I hope they see "life" as a miracle that is a gift from God and only God.

Hope has a whole new meaning in our family now. I pray this story touches your life in some way.

Angie Odom

"You are the God who performs miracles; you display

your power among the peoples."

Psalm 77:14

Chapter One

A Cold February Morning

I thought I had my day planned out. I arrived at the crisis pregnancy center I founded fourteen years ago, prepared for a typical day at work. I had arrived as normal and began getting the center ready for the day's clients and visitors. However, today was not going to be a typical day for me. I did not know it yet, but this day was going to change my life. Within minutes of arriving at the Center, I heard someone at the door. I went to the front lobby and I saw a lady standing outside on the sidewalk, holding a baby carrier. This was in the month of February, so it was cold outside. I invited her in, but she asked if I could take the baby inside while she got some things from the vehicle. I took the baby carrier - which was covered with a homemade pink blanket - went inside and sat it down on the couch in the front lobby. I wondered whose child this was, because the age of the lady at the door indicated it was not her child. I then uncovered the car seat and I saw a tiny little baby girl looking up at me. I could tell she was just a very young newborn because her skin still had wrinkles. She had a little bit of brown hair and big dark brown eyes. I just sat and talked to her while we waited on the woman to step inside.

The lady came back from the car and introduced herself as the child's grandmother. I will call her Irene in this book. She asked if I remembered her but I didn't. She then spoke about her daughter, whom I will call Marie. She said her daughter had once been a client of our Center and she asked if I remembered Marie. I immediately said I did, and

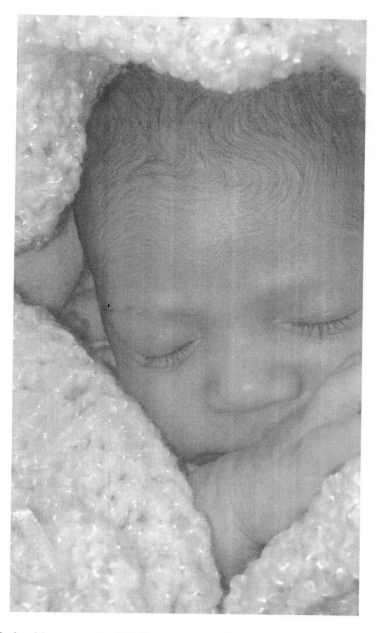

Baby Hope on that February morning when we first met.

asked where Marie was and how she was doing. Irene said "That's why I'm here - I need you to help me locate her and the last I heard the hospital sent her to Tennessee to a nursing home." I felt really confused about why this young lady, who was in her twenties, would be in a nursing home. Irene then explained that Marie's life had taken a turn for the worse a few years ago.

My mind went back nearly 10 years earlier to late 2003... back to meeting Marie. She was a beautiful, young girl with long dark hair, green eyes that had a mischievous twinkle to them and she always had a smile on her face. I first met Marie when she was 17. I was teaching an abstinence class at our local girls group home. The class talked about abstinence from sex, drugs and alcohol as well as how to develop rules and boundaries, and taking responsibility for your actions. The girls at this home all had troubled lives, and many of them had become involved in drugs at a young age. Members of her family had a history of drug use and Marie herself began using drugs by the age of 13.

Many of these girls at the home didn't come from stable family environments. Many longed for the interactions typical of a family and a sense of belonging. My daughter Bethany, who was about nine years old at the time, would often go with me to visit the girls. Some nights we would simply go and hang out with them and watch movies, just spending time with these young girls hoping to have a positive influence on their lives.

Some of the girls would come and volunteer at our Center - hanging up baby clothing and cleaning. One of those girls was Marie. We would sit and have long talks about her past drug problems and how she could remain positive in her life to battle her addiction. She would share with me how she couldn't wait to get out of the group home. She was hopeful about her future and wanted the opportunity to live her life. Shortly after Marie got out of the home she stopped coming by the Center.

When Marie was released from the group home, she received some money that her deceased father had left for her. Her father died when she was eight. He was a decorated combat veteran of World War II, having received the Purple Heart for injuries sustained in combat. When Marie was born her father was in his sixties and her mother was in her twenties. Marie had an older sister and an older brother – but she only shared a father with her brother.

Within months of leaving the group home, Marie had bought a car, crashed it, and ran through all of her money. People that never even checked on her while she was in the group home became her friends for a short while – but when the money was gone so were they. What Marie was left with was a drug addiction and a string of legal charges stemming from her drug and alcohol use.

One day out of the blue Marie showed up at the crisis pregnancy center. She had that sneaky smile on her face that I had missed seeing for some time. Marie said "Angie I have something to tell you".

Having operated the center for years, I had heard this sentence often, and of course I knew what was coming. She said she was pregnant and she wanted to know if our Center could help her. We sat and had what we called "our come to Jesus meeting" together where we had to talk about her drug use. She made a promise to lay down the drugs so her baby would be healthy. Marie attended our parenting classes and was doing good for a while, but she was still paying for all the trouble that had happened right after she got out of the group home. But, as had happened before, her visits became fewer until she stopped coming at all. I had no idea where she was or what she was into, but I was worried due to her history of drug use.

Our Center operated a jail ministry program where we witnessed to and worked with inmates in the local county jail. I had developed a point system where the female inmates could earn hygiene items by completing books and participating in our sessions. One day, in 2006, I was going from cell block to cell block at our local jail, sharing information with female inmates for our jail ministry program, and there stood Marie, smiling at me. I never would ask the girls why they were in jail or what their charges were. I left it up to them to share that information on their own if they chose to do so. But seeing Marie standing there, so far along in her pregnancy, I couldn't help myself. I asked her what she was doing in jail. She said she and her unborn child's father were on their way to get married when they were arrested. I laughed and jokingly told Marie I thought that was a sign she shouldn't get married. She told me she had been charged with writing bad checks or forging checks. I later learned that was not true, and that she was in jail for violating her probation on charges related to her drug and alcohol use and the crash she had shortly after leaving the group home. She asked me to help her get married because her baby was going to be born any day. I told her I didn't know what the jail would allow but I would check into it.

I went and spoke with my preacher, Pastor Joe Hensley, from Hunter Memorial Baptist Church. He was a young, on fire for the Lord preacher. He went and spoke to both of them and agreed to perform the marriage. The jail allowed for them to get married in a small room in the jail, but they couldn't touch one another. But I did bring a white sheet cake and plastic spoons! You would have thought by the smile on her face we were at a fancy wedding chapel and that this was her dream wedding.

It wasn't long after the wedding that her baby boy was born. I took a big gift basket of baby items and a bag of hygiene items for her to the hospital. She was so happy holding her baby boy. She talked about how she wanted to be a good mom, get a job and settle down. I prayed this would really happen. However, once again, our visits became fewer and fewer until they stopped all together and I lost contact with her. Knowing her past history, I once again became worried about her. I wondered how she was doing, how her baby was and I became afraid she had once again turned to the drugs that had all too often claimed a hold on her life.

One day out of the blue I got a call from her, when her baby was about three. She said she needed some help and asked if she could have some things she needed for her son. I told her the Center could help and I gathered up the items she needed. She never showed up to get them. That phone call was the last conversation I ever had with Marie.

As I sat there with Irene, while my mind was playing reruns of my past with Marie, I looked down wondering how this baby I was looking at played into this. Irene then told me Marie had been in Florida and had overdosed on drugs while she was pregnant. She said Marie was in a coma and after the baby had been born the hospital transferred Marie to a nursing home in Tennessee. Irene said she did not know what nursing home her daughter had been moved to but she gave me some phone numbers to try.

She told me the baby I was holding in my hands was Marie's child that had survived the overdose and the vegetative state until she could be born. Irene had gotten a court order to go to Pensacola, Florida, and take custody of Baby Hope. As I sat there listening to this story, with tears running down my face looking at this precious baby, I realized I was holding in my hands a miracle from God. At the time though, I did not understand the full extent of this miracle.

Irene then told me that she knew my family and remembered me from when I was a child. My father was a preacher and was over a bus ministry that would pick up children from the different neighborhoods and bring them to church. Irene told me when she was 9 years old she rode my parents church bus ministry. I was 5 years old at that time. One of the bus routes was driven by a man named Roy Blevins, and he drove the route which picked up Irene and her five siblings. My mother would visit the different bus routes and that is how she met Irene and her brothers and sisters. Irene said she remembered my parents taking her to church and she had great respect for my family. She said she also remembered how much I had helped Marie so she came to me for help because she knew she could count on me.

I asked how I could help and Irene said she needed eighteen dollars to send for Baby Hope's birth certificate, help setting up an appointment at the Department of Human Services to get insurance for Hope, and help getting Hope in at a pediatrician's office. I called and made an appointment for Hope to see a doctor, sent off for her birth certificate, made an appointment at DHS and gathered items from our Mommy Mart (the free store our Center operates for our clients) for Irene to use. We planned to go the next day to set up a nursery at Irene's apartment for Hope. I then started calling trying to find Marie and discovered the location where she was being cared for - a nursing home which was about three hours away from Elizabethton.

As I placed Hope back into her carseat, I was still so overwhelmed knowing what she had went through and knowing Marie was so sick. All I could do the rest of the day was cry and pray for God to show me what He wanted me to do to help.

The next day Tina Hagie and her daughter Hannah, both of whom volunteer at the Center, went with me to set up a nursery at Irene's apartment. Irene had some items needed for a baby that others had given her, but she did not even have a kitchen table or a bed for herself. Our Center was able to help out with these items. I helped carry Hope's items in and place them in her closet. I met a lady who was also helping place items in Hope's room. I found out later that she played a part in the story of what happened to Marie.

"Whoever oppresses the poor shows contempt for their Maker, but whoever is kind to the needy honors God." ~ Proverbs 14:31

Chapter Two
My Heart Breaks

The day after setting up the nursery for Irene, I left on my mission to find Marie. I traveled to the nursing home three hours away. A friend of mine named Jodi Buckles - and her kids Brayden, Jackson, and Madisyn - went with me. Jodi's husband Jack is on the Board of Directors for the Center and the two of them help out with our Center on a regular basis.

When we arrived at the nursing home, I had that awful feeling in the bottom of my stomach. I wanted to see her yet I didn't know how to prepare myself for her condition. I had to try to wipe away the tears and take a deep breath and go in. Marie needed me, but my heart was broken. I felt so many different emotions. Part of me was so angry at her for doing drugs, running from the police, leaving her son and prostituting to live. Another part was wanting to hug her and tell her everything was going to be okay. And a part of me felt guilty for the anger because I knew Marie was suffering the consequences of her choices already and what right did I have to be angry with her for her decisions.

As we walked down the hall I just kept pushing back the tears. I saw the room number and took a deep breath before walking in. I saw an older, grey-haired lady across the room in a bed. As I looked to my left, there on a thin mat on the floor, was Marie. They had mats around her and she kept rolling back and forth. My heart was crushed, all I could do was cry. She couldn't talk or respond to me. Her dark hair, which had always been so beautiful, was tangled. Her skin was so pale. Her feeding tube in her stomach kept swinging back and forth with each roll she made.

I went to get the nurse to ask her some questions and when I came back in the room Jackson, age 6, was sitting in the floor rubbing Marie's back. His heart is so kind and gentle to show the love of God to a woman he had never met. Most children would feel so uncomfortable in this setting, but not Jackson. He was doing the only thing he could think of to try to comfort someone.

When the nurse entered the room she sat in the floor with us and started explaining Marie's situation. The nursing home didn't know much about what happened to put Marie into their care. They knew she had suffered an overdose and also suffered from cerebral hypoxia - a condition which occurs due to decreased oxygen in the brain even though there is adequate blood flow. Cerebral Hypoxia can be brought on in a number of ways, one of which is overdose. There were a lot of unanswered questions. The staff at the nursing

Our first trip to see Marie in the nursing home

home said no one had been to visit her since she had arrived over a month earlier.

We laid down in the floor with her and tried to calm her from rolling back and forth, but nothing worked. They said she would roll out into the hall at times. One of her hands would continually move rubbing her chin. I knew the only answer was to try to get her moved closer to home so we could care for her. We spent the day in her room trying to provide her comfort and hoping to get a better understanding on her condition from her caregivers.

We circled up and took turns praying as we prepared to leave, with Brayden saying the final prayer. During our prayer, the older lady in the bed across the room tried to get up and it made her alarm go off. A nurse had come in during our prayer, but we didn't notice it. My phone went off and the ringtone played the words "My Verdict, Not Guilty". When we opened our eyes a young nurse was standing there, crying her eyes out. I asked her what was wrong but she said she couldn't tell us or she could lose her job. I walked over and shut the door and asked her to please tell us. I worried she knew something that no one wanted me to know about Marie. As she was wiped the tears from her face, she said "You don't understand. I'm 21 years old, a preacher's kid, and I am pregnant. My parents are going to kill me and their church will disown them. I had went and partied for my 21st birthday and became pregnant because of it." I said to her "Honey, you are not going to believe this, but I direct a crisis pregnancy center and this patient was one of our past clients. God has us here for a reason." Weeping she said all day she tried to stay away from our room because she felt God was convicting her heart. It was hearing Brayden's prayer - the heartfelt prayer of a 7-year-old child - that had touched her heart and made her realize how she needed to raise her child to know the Lord.

Jodi and I talked with her more, and we explained how God would forgive her and how He loves her. We prayed and she rededicated her life to Christ. As she left the room with a huge smile on her face and peace in her heart, I wondered if I was ever going to be able to speak to Marie like that again.

It was a long drive, leaving the nursing home. It was in the middle of nowhere. Leaving her there, so far from home, felt as if I was leaving my child behind all alone. She couldn't speak for herself and we were having to trust strangers to care for her. I knew I had to get back home and find a place that would take her.

When I returned home, I met with Marie's mother and explained to her what we had been told. We both agreed we needed to get her closer to home. I started calling local nursing homes, and after the ninth one turned me down I knew if I didn't get some help this move wasn't going to happen. Many of the nursing homes told me she didn't have the right type of insurance or that a full assessment would need to be completed before she could be admitted. Some even told me they would not accept her, even with a complete assessment, because her condition was drug related and she had a history of drug abuse. I just kept praying for God to show me which way to turn for help.

Still without an answer, the next week I made the three hour journey to check on Marie. My friend Nikki Winters, who volunteers at our Center, went with me. When I walked into Marie's room my heart dropped and my blood pressure hit the roof. She was lying on a thin mat on the floor, with most of her body exposed. She was covered with dried feces from head to toe. Her hair was tangled, matted and so oily it looked wet from not being washed. Her lungs had a rattle to them. She was in bad shape. I immediately took pictures and asked Nikki to wait with her while I went to get help.

I went to the main office and asked for the Nursing Home Administrator to come to Marie's room with me. When I walked her back and showed her how Marie looked, and the lack of care, she agreed it was not acceptable. She told me she would see to it that Marie would get the care she needed. She called for nurses to bathe Marie, and x-rays were ordered for her chest to check for pneumonia. I went out in the hall and called a man I know who had experience operating nursing homes. I explained what was going on and asked what I should do. He told me some of the things I needed to do in order to get her moved and what I needed to do immediately to correct the problem at that facility.

I let the nursing home administrator know I would be reporting Marie's condition and the lack of care to the state and I would be removing Marie from their facility as soon as I found another facility to accept her. The next day I called our local nursing homes again trying to find a facility to take her. They all told me the same thing. Marie didn't have the right kind of insurance to help determine if she needs therapy or not and that a full assessment was required to be considered for admission.

All I could do was just cry out to God and pray He would show me what to do. I felt so helpless. Here was a woman who could not care for herself, could not even speak for herself, and no one cared enough to even consider her basic human dignity. No one took the time to care for her, bathe her or brush her hair. She was like a helpless child with one difference - people feel empathy for a child. The impression I was left with was that many people felt no empathy for Marie because her condition was one of her own making through her choices and her drug use.

The next day I woke up feeling that God laid it on my heart that I needed to contact a congressman or someone higher up who has some pull. It was then that I called Representative Phil Roe, who is a U.S. Congressman. He is also not only a doctor, but an obstetrics and gynecology doctor who has delivered countless children. He had always told me if our Center ever needed him to call. We never had called him before, but on this day I knew we needed him. I called his cell phone and he immediately answered. When I shared with him what little I knew at that point, he was shocked that the baby had survived the circumstances of her birth. I remember he kept asking me "are you sure the baby is alive" and when I finally convinced him that the baby had survived and I had seen it, he simply asked "what do you need?"

I explained our concerns with not only Marie's health issues but also with the conditions at the nursing home where we found her. When I told him the conditions we had seen and the lack of care we had witnessed, he said the situation definitely needed to be reported. But, he said, we needed to get Marie out of the nursing home first before we reported it. He felt Marie's health was in serious jeopardy at that facility and without proper care she could die. I told him the local nursing homes had refused to accept Marie because she needed a rehabilitation assessment. A friend of mine, Lisa Lyons, had tried to secure an assessment through the Quillen Rehabilitation Center but was told Marie did not have the correct type of insurance for their facility. Congressman Roe then said the most hopeful words I had heard yet in dealing with this situation. He said "Give me 24 hours. I am going to see what I can do and I will get back in touch with you." True to his word he called me back, and in less than the 24 hours he had asked for. He had worked with Brian Huff, the director of Quillen Rehabilitation Center, and had gotten it approved for the rehabilitation center to accept Marie. I was so happy and relieved, but I knew the next obstacle would be transportation.

I called the nursing home where she was at and was told they did not have transportation available but they might be able to find a van and driver if I would ride in the back of the van with her. Even with my lack of medical knowledge, I knew this was not the proper way to transport someone with a serious medical condition from one nursing home to another.

After speaking with the nursing home, I brought this situation up to our Center's board of directors and one of the board members – Jack Buckles, who is our local Fire Marshal – said he would contact our local emergency medical service to see if they could transport her. He called and spoke with Anthony Roberts, with the Carter County Rescue Squad, and the only question he asked was if Marie was from Carter County. When he was told she was he simply said "Then we'll go get her. We don't leave our own behind." Even after learning that Marie's insurance would not cover the cost of the transport, the Carter County Rescue Squad still made the trip to get her and bring her back to East Tennessee - knowing they would never receive payment for their services.

"I will lift up my eyes to the hills from whence cometh my help." ~ Psalm 121:1

Chapter Three
A Late Night Phone Call

As I was working through the details of getting Marie transferred to a local nursing home, our story took another turn. One night – somewhere around 10:30 p.m. – my husband and Bethany were already in bed. My daughter had her own apartment, but she wasn't feeling well and had come to stay at our home for the night. I myself was getting ready for bed when my phone rang. It was Irene. She said "We have a problem." She told me she was at the office for the Department of Children's Services. A caseworker from DCS had visited Irene's home that day after receiving an anonymous tip that there was possible drug activity in the home while an infant was present. Irene told me she spoke with the caseworker during the investigation. While the caseworker was completing the home visit, several red flags came up and the caseworker asked Irene to come to the DCS office for a formal visit. Irene said she had been honest and told them she had "taken something" for her nerves which had not been prescribed for her. She said "I don't understand why that's a problem," and she just kept saying that to me over and over. She told me DCS was removing Hope from her care and wanted to place the baby with someone else temporarily.

During the placement process, DCS checked several members of the family to see if they would be suitable for the placement of an infant but the other family members could not pass the background check. DCS could not find a family member whom they felt was a good placement for such a small infant with the special needs that Hope had due to the circumstances of her birth.

Irene said she hated to ask me if I could take care of Hope, but wanted to know if I would be willing to take care of her "just for a little while." She again reminded me of how long she had known my family, how she had so much respect for my parents and how I had helped Marie through her first pregnancy and at other times in Marie's life. She asked me to please take Hope and care for her while DCS was working on the case. I told her we would agree to take care of Hope for as long as we were needed.

The DCS case worker then called us to get our information so he could do a background check on us. He said he would call us back, and within a short time he called and said he would be bringing Hope to us and he would be at our home within half an hour. I then went into the bedroom and woke Earl up. I said "Honey, they are bringing us a baby to take care of for a while." He asked me if he needed to get up and I told him I was sure there would be papers for us to sign. I also went and woke up Bethany and told her they were bringing a baby that needed care to our home. It took a little while for her to wake up and really understand what was happening. I also called my mother, who lives next door, and let her know what was going on and that a baby was on the way to our house. It was a whole family affair for us, getting our support network together. I also sent out a text to our prayer group to let them know a baby was being brought to our home from DCS and asking that they pray for the situation and our family.

A short time later I heard the DCS caseworker pull into our driveway and in my tired state of mind I thought "And people say there is no such thing as a stork and here is one with four wheels" and I laughed to myself. I began asking the caseworker questions about the baby, when she had last eaten, what her sleeping patterns were like, when the last time she had used the bathroom was. He looked at me and said "I'm sorry, I don't have that information. I do know what kind of formula she drinks." The paperwork from DCS said Hope had been removed from Irene's care on an immediate protective order because it was determined Irene could not care for the baby at that time. Hope had been in Irene's care for around 20 days when DCS removed her from the home. Hope was so little she was wearing a newborn sleeper with a little bear and polka dots on it. She had a handmade blanket, a small diaper bag and a bottle.

At this point I realized I didn't have anything in the home to care for a baby. Bethany was 21 years old at this time and she was the last baby that had been in our home. Even though I operate a crisis pregnancy center and I work with baby items all the time, I typically don't keep those things at home. I called Jack and Jodi Buckles, somewhat in a panic, and asked them if they could go to our Center and pick up some things for us just to get through the night until I could go to the store and pick up the things we needed. My biggest concern was getting something for her to sleep in – a bed or a bassinet – but she ended up sleeping in my arms because she was in such an emotional state.

Jack and Jodi went to the Center and got the items we needed and brought them to our home. They arrived shortly after the DCS case worker left. When they got here, we all prayed, and cried, and comforted Hope and each other. It was a very emotional time for our family and for Jack and Jodi as well. They had both played such a large part in Hope and Marie's lives in the past few weeks – from seeing Hope for the first time and going to see Marie in the nursing home and working to get her transferred to a local facility. After a time, Jack and Jodi left our house to return to their home, and I remember thinking to myself I didn't know what I was going to do. I couldn't help but feel so much emotion knowing Marie was lying in the nursing home and now her baby was in my arms in a crisis situation. I remember I felt guilty because I was getting to comfort Hope, something Marie would never get to do. I wanted to cry and get my feelings out but I knew Hope needed me to be strong and help her. Through the night she cried and jerked even though she was in my arms. Her nose would sound congested each time she would have a bottle. I couldn't wait for daylight so I could get suggestions on caring for Hope. We thought maybe she had colic.

I went to work at the center the next morning, after having gotten very little sleep, and I took Hope to work with me. I had to teach a parenting class for our clients and I remember laughing at the irony of teaching a parenting class when I had just spent the night with a child I could not get to go to sleep.

That day Gracen King, one of our Center's volunteers, came to work and met Hope. Gracen was one of the people we had texted asking for prayer. During the day I went to the store to look for some of the items we would need for Hope, and Gracen went with me. That evening, Gracen showed up at our home with her parents, Pastor Alan King and his wife Shelley. I was surprised to see them come to my house, but I was even more surprised by what they brought with them. They had gone to a store in Johnson City and had purchased a new stroller/carseat combo, a new pack-and-play set-up that had a bassinet, a new baby swing, diapers and a variety of other odds and ends you need when there is a baby in the home. I remember telling them I wasn't sure if we were going to have her for long because I was told it was a temporary situation. They said it did not matter how long she was with me, the baby needed these items wherever she was. They said their church, Zion Baptist where he pastored, wanted to purchase these items.

While the King family was at the store purchasing these items, they shared what they knew of Hope's story, that she was in need and had been removed from her home by DCS, and the store gave them a discount. An employee from that store met the King family and said she had been touched by this situation and gave them a gift card for Hope.

All I could do was cry because I was so touched by their generosity. Many other wonderful and loving people came to support us and assist us with the challenge God had set before us. Looking back I see now that God was showing me that while He was leading me on this new adventure in my life I should put my trust in Him to help provide. Like the saying goes – If God brings you to it, He will bring you through it.

It felt so odd to be on the other side of this situation. For fourteen years I have taken items to families in need. They would thank me and tell me how much it meant to them. I now know first hand because I was so thankful and touched by the kindness that was shown to me. It reaffirmed what an important role the Center plays in moments like these.

Earl holding Hope shortly after she came to live with us

"I wait for the Lord, my soul waits, and in his word I put my hope." - Psalm 130:5

Chapter Four
Marie And Hope Meet

The day arrived that we were bringing Marie back to East Tennessee. By this point, Hope had been living with us for two days. My friends and volunteers Kristie Carr and Jodi Buckles went with me to the rehabilitation center. We arrived early, praying that all would go well. Anthony Roberts himself went on the trip to pick up Marie and bring her home. Along with Anthony went an emergency medical worker named Jeff White, who also works with the Carter County Rescue Squad. Both of those men were so caring in transporting Marie. They called us numerous times during the trip to update us and let us know that Marie was ok.

Jeff & Anthony with Hope the day of the transport

After the transport, I had the opportunity to speak with Anthony about the ride back. Anthony said during the transport there were two times where the ambulance was brought to a halt due to traffic - the first time due to a wreck and the second time due to construction where the road was being paved. Each of these stops put the transport behind schedule. As the trip went on, Anthony said Marie became agitated and began trying to roll and flail her arms and legs. This happened because her medication was wearing off.

Anthony said at first they tried to calm her with music from the radio. He said that worked for a while, but after so long sitting in traffic even that stopped soothing her. Anthony said Jeff began singing to Marie and that proved to be even more calming than the radio. Anthony said Jeff loves to sing and on that trip he thought Jeff must have sung every song he knew. It touched me that these men would care so much about a total stranger that one of them would spend hours singing to her just to bring her comfort.

When they arrived at the rehabilitation center, we realized the nursing home Marie had been in had failed to send her medical records with her. At this point in time we still knew very little about what had happened to her and the extent of the medical issues she was facing. We knew she had overdosed and was in a vegetative state, but that was just about all we knew. I went outside and met Marie as they were getting her out of the ambulance. I talked to her to let her know she was going to be okay and that I was there.

On the day Marie was transferred to Quillen Rehab Center, Irene was supposed to meet us there to help get her checked in. I had called Irene about an hour before the ambulance arrived with Marie to let her know what time the ambulance would be at the rehabilitation center. She was not there when Marie arrived. Irene said she had to wait for her sister to pick her up. They arrived four hours late. It quickly became apparent that Irene was not able to handle the medical situation with her daughter. Irene had told me before that she does have several health issues - including prior strokes. In talking to the family it did not seem like they were very interested in the care of Marie. Because of the lack of support from Marie's family, I found myself being made the surrogate decision maker for Marie. Even though I was only given responsibility for the decisions about her medical care, it was a very emotional and overwhelming situation for me.

Perhaps the most emotional part of that day for me was getting to see Marie and Hope reunited. It was the first time the two of them had been in the same room since Hope had been delivered by C-section. We took Hope into Marie's room. As was normal, Marie was rolling back and forth endlessly in her bed. I held Hope down beside the bed and told Marie her baby was there. Jodi kept saying "snuggle your baby Marie, snuggle your baby". Marie rolled toward Hope and began to cry, tears running down her face. After that encounter, it was almost as if a peace came over her. Her constant rolling, which had been an ever-present part of her condition up until this point, stopped. That was the only time I have ever seen a response from Marie since her overdose. Even though I have continued to take Hope to see her birth mother, we have not seen a response like this since that first time. Marie doesn't cry, and she doesn't roll back and forth anymore. There have never been any tears like we saw at that moment. Kristie was able to photograph and video that reunion between Marie and Hope while Jodi and I comforted the both of them. I really feel that God did that. He allowed that response from Marie, so I could have it on

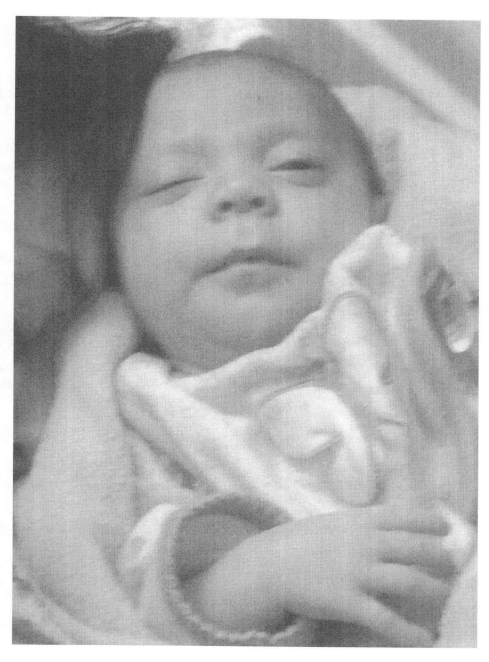

Marie & Hope the day they were reunited

video to show Hope when she grows up, so she will know her mother did love her.

While Marie was at Quillen Rehabilitation Center we learned a lot more about her condition. We were able to get medical records from the hospital in Pensacola, Florida, where Marie had been treated and Hope had been born - Sacred Heart Hospital. We learned the extent of the damage Marie's brain had sustained through the Cerebral Hypoxia, which is a condition that occurs when the brain is deprived of oxygen. Brain cells are extremely sensitive to oxygen deprivation and can begin to die within five minutes after the oxygen supply has been cut off. When hypoxia lasts for longer periods of time, it can cause coma, seizures, and even brain death. We learned Marie's brain had been without the proper levels of oxygen for approximately four hours. Marie had been placed on life support while at the hospital.

Irene told us the doctors at the hospital wanted to remove Marie from life support while she was being treated at Sacred Heart Hospital, but she refused to allow it. Irene said the doctors told her the baby had no chance of survival but still she refused. Marie was on life support for about two and a half months. Once doctors were able to control Marie's seizures, she began rolling from side to side. The rolling became almost uncontrollable. The nurses who cared for Marie later told me there were days where her body did not stop rolling to sleep.

While at the rehabilitation center, doctors did a wide variety of tests on all sorts of different brain functions and abilities. They checked everything they could think of to test. The therapy teams were wonderful and went out of their way to try to help Marie. The doctors determined Marie was in what they described as a "persistent vegetative" state. One doctor said a newborn infant had more response reactions than Marie did. We were told Marie had sustained total damage to her brain and brain stem. We were told she was completely blind but still had her hearing. One doctor said unless there was a miracle Marie would remain in that condition. He did not see any other hope for improvement. They had exhausted all efforts, but said they would help in getting her placed in a long-term care facility. I was thankful for all the help I received in getting this all-important evaluation for Marie, because accomplishing this would have been impossible on my own. We were able to get her placed in a local nursing home.

"Fear them not therefore: for there is nothing covered, that shall not be revealed; and hid, that shall not be known." ~ Matthew 10:26

Chapter Five
Learning The Truth

It was so hard to get the true facts or information on what really went on in Florida from Irene. Even though she is now only 49 years old, Irene has had two strokes. She cannot drive. She also has short term memory loss due to her strokes. Sometimes I would feel like she and the other family members knew more than what they were telling me about Marie's life and what had really happened. I quickly decided that if I wanted to know what had happened I would have to find out on my own. As I learned more of the situation Irene would share a little more information or confirm what I had learned, but the vast majority of what I now know about what happened to Marie I found through my own investigations. At first I had been afraid to research the situation, afraid of what I would learn. But God put that fear at ease and reminded me I needed to learn what had happened to Marie so I would know how to help Hope. So I continued my research. What I learned broke my heart.

This vibrant young woman I had gotten to know at so many points in her life had succumbed to her addiction. The choices she made robbed her of the life she could have had.

As had happened so many times in her life, Marie had turned to drugs once again. As I began to learn more about Marie's home life and family structure, it became less surprising that drugs had taken over her life. Marie was not the only member of her family who battled a substance abuse problem.

I found out Marie had fled from our area. She was on the run, hiding from the police. There were outstanding warrants for her arrest. She had left her young son behind. She had been arrested numerous times in our county, as well as in surrounding areas and states. Her charges ranged from shoplifting, theft and driving under the influence to drug possession, evading arrest and assault on an officer. Those are only a few of the many charges I learned Marie had been arrested for.

To help get out of her own legal trouble, Marie provided information to law enforcement officers on other people, something called "snitching" among those involved in the drug culture. Marie had provided information to the police regarding crimes other people had committed. This is a very unpopular thing among people in the drug culture, and it can be very dangerous for those who do it. Marie found herself not only being looked for by the police, but also being targeted by people in the drug community - the community in which she had spent most of her life. She feared for her safety. For a time she would not leave her own home because of that fear. She eventually fled the area with a friend, and it appears she left not a moment too soon. The day after she left, her home was riddled with bullets.

Marie and her friend ended up in Pensacola, Florida. I later found out the mother of the friend she fled with had taken the two of them to Pensacola, handed them some cash and dropped them off. She then returned to Tennessee, leaving Marie and her son behind. I also later learned the friend's mother was the same woman I had met the day I was helping set up a nursery for Hope at Irene's apartment.

Drugs had completely taken over Marie's life at this time. When the money ran out, Marie turned to other ways to support her drug habit. She ended up working as a prostitute in order to get the money she needed to buy drugs. Her drug dealer, who ended up having a sexual relationship with her, became her pimp. Marie would walk the streets barefoot, selling herself in order to obtain her next high. She was arrested at least once while in Pensacola. When she was taken to the hospital suffering from the overdose, the bottoms of her feet were in terrible shape from walking barefoot on the hot pavement in Florida.

I learned from speaking to police officers and requesting copies of police reports, that Marie had been living in an extended stay motel at the time of her overdose. I was told the motel was known for drug trafficking and prostitution. Her drug dealer was the person who called 911 to report the overdose. He told police he came into the hotel room and found her unconscious and unresponsive on the floor. I learned when he called 911 he gave them the wrong name for the hotel they were staying at - a move which sent paramedics responding to a location across town from where they actually were. I was told by emergency personnel this delayed help reaching Marie by approximately 30 minutes.

After some time, the man finally gave the dispatcher the correct name of the hotel and paramedics were able to arrive in time to save Marie's life. When the paramedics who responded learned Marie was pregnant - something she herself had learned only two days before - they checked her blood sugar level and it registered 11. The normal range for a blood sugar check on a person who has not eaten is between 70 and 100. When blood sugar levels drop below 70 a condition called hypoglycemia occurs. If the number drops well below 70 it can result in seizures, coma or even death. Marie was transported by ambulance to Sacred Heart Hospital for treatment.

The investigator's report states that Marie was found on the floor face down. Several people who were at the hotel were interviewed by police, and they had conflicting stories. One person said Marie had gone out the night before to look for bath salts - a synthetic drug comparable to meth used to obtain a high - and stole some medication called Adderall from a friend. Adderall is a prescription medication used to treat Attention Deficit Disorder and narcolepsy which is sometimes abused by those with addiction issues. Another witness said Marie had taken a pill she believed to be Xanax on the day of her overdose, but the witness thought it might have actually been a prescription blood pressure medication.

Marie's brother Aaron - who was also living in Florida at this time and running from the law - told Irene that Marie had gotten the beating that was meant for her pimp. The police report and hospital reports did not note any physical injuries sustained by Marie that would have been consistent with being beaten. During the investigation, police were not able to locate Aaron and speak to him about what he told his mother because he had fled the area after Marie's overdose.

Marie was placed on life support. It was determined she had suffered a poly-substance overdose - which means there were multiple drugs in her system which contributed to the overdose. Police said it was not clear if she had taken the drugs herself or if someone else had forced her to take the drugs. She began suffering from severe seizures, a condition common to those addicted to drugs when they begin detoxing. Marie spent two and half months on life support. She recovered

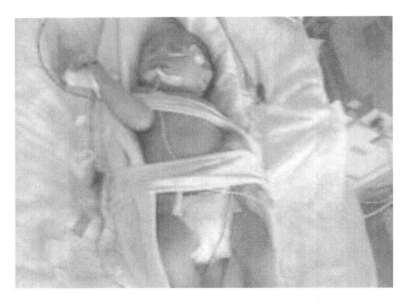

Hope was cared for in the NICU at Sacred Heart

enough to be removed from life support, but she was kept on a regimen of medication to control her seizures. For the remainder of her pregnancy Marie remained in this same hospital in a vegetative state.

Hope was born six weeks early by C-section delivery. Doctors delivered the baby early due to pregnancy complications caused by her mother's condition. Marie was suffering from preeclampsia, which is a pregnancy complication characterized by high blood pressure and signs of damage to other organ systems, oftentimes the kidneys. Left untreated, preeclampsia can lead to serious, even fatal, complications for both mother and baby.

Marie was also suffering from low levels of amniotic fluid - which is the fluid which surrounds the baby in the womb and serves as part of the baby's life support system. Marie also suffered from grade 2 placenta infections - also known as major grade placenta infections. The umbilical cord had also become wrapped around Hope's neck. All of those conditions can be very harmful to mother and baby, but our God is a God of miracles. Despite all of the odds and all of the problems, Hope continued to grow and develop in her mother's womb.

Three days after the C-section Marie was sent to the nursing home. Hope had to detox from the medical drugs which had been used to care for Marie. She remained in the hospital's neo-natal intensive care unit for 23 days. Hope was then released to the custody of her grandmother, Irene, which is where I became a part of her story.

"Find rest, O my soul, in God alone; my hope comes from him." - Psalm 62:5

Chapter Six
A Whole New World

Once Earl and I became the temporary caregivers of Hope, we soon realized we were going to have to learn to be parents all over again. Hope was facing situations in her young life that we had never encountered.

Hope had never bonded with a parent the way most babies do. She was born by C-section to a mother who was in a vegetative state. Her mother could not hold her, feed her, comfort her, soothe her or bond with her. Hope was in a neonatal intensive care unit where she had no interactions with her family. I learned that during the entire time Hope was in the hospital in Florida, no family member ever visited. The only daily support Hope had was from the hospital staff. It saddens me to think she was going through so much without having one constant person there each day for her.

I learned I was caring for a child who was suffering the effects of detoxing - something called Neonatal Abstinence Syndrome (NAS) - and who could be facing a myriad of other health issues. It became obvious that Hope was suffering with some sensory issues so we began making appointments with doctors to find out how we could best get her treatment. We enrolled her in the Tennessee Early Intervention Services program. We saw a specialist in neurology.

Because so little is known about the long-term effects of NAS, we were increasingly concerned of what may happen to Hope. We didn't know what to expect, and I feel the doctor's really did not know either. I also think that, at times, the doctors would hear about Hope's history and the circumstances of her birth and would look to find something wrong, because they just could not believe that a baby who had survived all that Hope did could be healthy. But every time a doctor would say one thing, God would say something else. We were told many different conditions Hope could be suffering from - ranging from cerebral palsy to club foot. But every time there was bad news, God proved He is a healer.

Hope has faced some developmental issues. She underwent physical therapy. She is still going through occupational therapy and speech therapy. However, these issues are similar to what other children born premature experience. The problems Hope has experienced are nothing compared to what they could have been or what we were told they may be.

As soon as Hope came into our home I knew I needed to take her to the doctor to make sure I was meeting her needs with food and to find out why she would arch her back and cry when we were feeding her. She would not spit up but throw up... a lot. The problem was when she would throw up it wouldn't come out, it just stayed in her throat and mouth. I would have to turn her face towards the floor each time that would happen. Nighttime was the worst. She cried a lot, but the scary part was worrying if she was going to choke or aspirate, which is a condition that occurs when a person throws up but is unable to clear their mouth so the fluid is pulled into the lungs and the person chokes to death. I knew this baby had every caution symptom for Sudden Infant Death Syndrome, which worried me, but her risk for aspiration made it even scarier. I had a bassinet next to my bed with an insert underneath the mattress so one end was higher, but still if she spit up she would lay there with it in her mouth. I decided the only way to make sure she would not aspirate was to hold her with her head at my shoulder, her body straight down my arm and use pillows behind me so I was sitting straight up. I didn't want to use a blanket around her face so I cut the hood off a soft outfit that was made to go over babies when they go out into the cold. I would just put that on her with a diaper.

This is how I slept for the first six months that Hope was in our home. Hope would not lay down for any length of time without beginning to scream. She would be asleep and then, out of no where, a scream - not a cry, but a scream - that would make the hair on your neck stand up. We were given a co-sleeper to put in the bed with us from Zion Baptist Church. We put that in the bed and even took one of our thicker Bibles and put under the little pad in it so it would be at a tilt. We also prayed for God to provide her with peace through His word.

When she would drink her bottle her nose would stop up and have a rattle. Hope would sneeze a lot. The only way to truly keep her asleep was to swing her. The normal baby swing didn't do the trick. I mean swinging her by bending your knees up and down and moving side to side. The way she wanted to be moved would have scared my first born, but to Hope it was comfort. I looked at it as a new workout plan that caused me to lose over 10 lbs. in the first few weeks. My husband and I took turns walking the floors at night with her. If she was asleep she would wake up as soon as the movement would stop.

We understand this behavior now, but then we just didn't know what caused it. Her legs would stiffen up to the point that when I would dress her in sleepers, I had to put her feet in first. Bath time from the start was so hard for her. It seemed anything that touched her skin made her cry. I couldn't rub lotion on her or wash her with a washcloth, she would cry because it hurt her. I could only wrap a towel lightly around her and give her time to dry without patting her with the towel. She would be asleep and her arms or legs would jerk so bad it would scare me to death. We would want to cuddle and hold her tight against us but her little body would push away. We tried the blankets like the NICU nurses use to swaddle her, but the confinement of the blanket seemed to terrify her. If she couldn't move her arms her screams would become louder. She wouldn't take a pacifier. She would try to suck her whole hand but had trouble with a pacifier. She would break out into sweats to the point of being so soaked that I would have to change her clothes.

At this time I was also taking care of Hope's birth mother Marie. During one visit to the rehab center where Marie was being evaluated I talked to a physical therapist and I explained to her what was going on. She held Hope and said it could be that she had some in-depth disabilities because of her tendency to arch her back and cry. I just knew we had to get to the bottom of what made her hurt and unhappy. I took her back to the pediatrician that Irene and I had previously taken Hope to in order to try to explain these behaviors and problems we were seeing. I asked them to send for the birth records from Florida because I only had three pieces of paper from there which Irene had given me, and they did not explain very much. I felt as if they did not listen to what I was trying to explain to them. They did order a swallow test but I had to call back three times to get it scheduled.

When I arrived a week later for this swallow test the orders were wrong and did not include the speech therapist that needed to attend. But a sweet dedicated speech therapist at the hospital said she would stand in anyway. After the test she offered for us to go upstairs where she could try to feed Hope. She didn't know how much I just wanted to hug her and cry on her shoulder, just because she said she wanted to take a closer look. After feeding her she did recommend for Hope to be treated for reflux. During the test the sound of her food all going into her nose was bad. I became even more worried about Hope and the problems she was having eating. I called the doctor's office and waited for days to hear back. They had problems finding the results, but eventually Hope was put on medication to treat her reflux problem.

"Be joyful in hope, patient in affliction, faithful in prayer." ~ Romans 12:12

Chapter Seven
Three words that changed our lives - Neonatal Abstinence Syndrome

Neonatal Abstinence Syndrome (NAS) is a medical condition which has only been recognized in the last couple of years. Because it had been undiagnosed before - and really had not been viewed as a specific medical condition - not a lot of information is available on NAS or the problems it can cause for children. Many doctors are just now seeing this condition and are having to learn how to treat it on their own since little research is available. NAS occurs because a pregnant woman takes drugs - illegal or prescription - during her pregnancy and the baby is born suffering the effects of withdrawal from the drug. During the pregnancy, the drugs pass through the placenta that connects the baby to its mother in the womb. The baby becomes addicted along with the mother. At birth, the baby is still dependent on the drug, but because the baby is no longer in the womb and getting the drug from the mother, symptoms of withdrawal occur.

I founded a crisis pregnancy center 14 years ago. Throughout the years I have worked with many clients who have had substance abuse problems. The first time I ever heard the words "Neonatal Abstinence Syndrome" was after beginning to care for Hope. The reason NAS is coming to the forefront now and getting so much attention is because of the drug crisis facing our nation. Even though drug use has been a problem for decades, there was no research into what affect drugs would have on pregnant women or their children in the womb.

NAS has become so prolific that on January 1, 2013, the State of Tennessee declared it a "reportable condition" and required that all hospitals, birthing centers and healthcare providers report instances of the diagnosis to the Tennessee Department of Health. In 2013, the first year which reporting was mandatory, there were 855 cases of NAS reported in Tennessee.

Even though it is now mandatory to report a diagnosis of NAS in Tennessee, there is still very limited information available about the long-term effects a child may suffer from being exposed to drugs in the womb. Many developmental issues in children take some time - ranging from months to years - to show up. I am sharing this information in this book because I believe it is important to share the story of all Hope went through - and that includes NAS. Many individuals are like me and had never heard of NAS, and I feel it is important to tell about this condition so others can learn about it.

"I can do all things through Christ who strengthens me." ~ *Philippians 4:13*

Chapter Eight
Temporary Becomes More Permanent

During this same time of getting evaluations and therapies lined up for Hope, I had a meeting at the DCS office regarding Hope. Irene had been instructed to gather reports from her doctors regarding her medical conditions and prescription medications. She was also instructed to bring paperwork from her doctor stating that she was healthy enough to care for a baby. Submitting to the testing and bringing in the requested medical records were going to be a condition of Irene regaining custody of Hope. Rather than going through all of the DCS conditions, Irene said she would agree that she was not able to care for the baby, and she began to work with DCS to develop a care plan for Hope. Irene called me and told me that she didn't feel she could take care of Hope, and she asked if my husband and I would agree to permanently raise her. My husband and I agreed to pray to see if this was God's will for this child and for us. He was 48 at the time and I was 42. My daughter Bethany was grown, had moved out into her own place and was about to get married. My step-son was married and already had a child. We also worried if we knew how to help her properly with her medical condition.

While my husband and I were praying over this situation to see what direction God would lead us, there came a day where I had to take Hope for a doctor's appointment. My mother went along with me. She had never voiced her opinion to me about whether or not Earl and I should raise Hope. While we were driving to the appointment, my mother said "Have you ever considered that maybe God wants you to raise this child?" I told my mother that God would need to show me a big sign to help me understand this was His will. Earl and I had never discussed or even considered adoption. We helped other families with their adoptions, but it was just never something we considered for ourselves. While driving on the old Johnson City highway - and just seconds after I told my mother I would need a sign from God - on the left side of the road I saw a sign that said "Angela's House of Hope." My real first name is Angela, but no one ever calls me that. Seeing the sign kind of blew my mind and my mother turned to me and said, "Well Angie, there's your sign." God has such an amazing sense of humor. I laughed because I remembered a similar situation which happened 14 years ago when God was laying it on my heart to start the women's center ministry. I had been giving God all the excuses which I could think of not to start the Center - I didn't know how to do it, we didn't have the money to get started. While I was driving down the road talking to God about it, I looked to my right and saw a bumper sticker that said "I can do all things through Jesus Christ who strengthens me."

After seeing the sign that said Angela's House of Hope I turned to my mom laughing and said "It's going to take a bigger sign than that." Well, the Bible says ask and ye shall receive.I had driven less than a mile when I passed a sign on the right side of the road advertising insurance. It said "Do you have your family covered?" It made me immediately think about Hope and whether or not she was meant to be part of our family. I then passed a third, this one on the left side of the road. It said "Is your child in the right car seat?" That made me think about if Hope was where she was supposed to be. I laughed and said "Ok, I get it Lord."

That night I was walking the floor with Hope and a confirmation from God came over me and I felt His peace cover me. With my tears dripping onto Hope's face, I told her how much love I felt for her and gave my excuses over to God. I know He placed the love that a mother has for a child in my heart for Hope. I then said "God if this child is to be raised in our family then you will need to show my husband this is Your will because we have to be

Bethany, Earl and I with Hope at her baby shower.

together as one to raise her and serve You."

Within 24 hours of my prayer my husband agreed that we needed to accept the request from the grandmother to raise Hope. I called to let our caseworker know and he had us meet him two days later to sign custody papers. We were then granted full custody of Hope. All of this - from Hope being brought to our home that first night, reaching the temporary custody order and finally the permanent custody agreement - occurred in less than one month.

About a month after Earl and I were granted permanent custody, Hunter Memorial Baptist Church, where our family attended, and some of our friends held a baby shower for Hope. We wanted to help make memories and pictures that we could share with Hope later in life showing how many people love her. Our Center was completing construction on the new part of our building. I never imagined the first event in the TLC Community Center part would be a baby shower for a baby in our home.

I switched Hope to a different doctor's office around this time because I felt we were not making progress or getting the help Hope needed, and I called to get enrolled with Tennessee Early Intervention and made an appointment for them to see Hope. They came out to our home and did evaluations on everything about her. Misty came to sign her up and work on some things and then another lady came to do her hearing and vision screenings. Hope did meet the guidelines for this program and was considered high risk due to her time in the womb and conditions surrounding her birth. I can't say enough about how wonderful this program is. It helped our family tremendously. They were wonderful with Hope and very encouraging to us. They would hold her, work with her, and then share goals that we needed to work on between therapy sessions. I still use Tennessee Early Intervention today, and Hope is nineteen months old. They come to my workplace to do their visit with Hope now. They helped send me to the right people Hope needed to see along the way and I feel they are part of our family. Hope cries for Misty when she walks in the doors. They have gone out of their way to help and I will be forever grateful.

Along with TEI we see Dr. Higginbotham, who is Hope's pediatrician. She has been wonderful from day one. I remember the first day she saw Hope and I had to tell the history on her. She just sat and listened without trying to hurry to her next patient. She has always listened to my concerns and ordered tests when needed without question. As a mom I would go in overwhelmed with concern and she would say "this is normal" or "let's don't worry about that right now, I feel she is going to overcome that." Just the calm in her voice and the reassurance meant so much. The staff there was so kind. They didn't look at Hope as just some drug addict's baby.

Trust me, until you go through this you don't understand how many people would say things like "You better not keep that baby, you don't know what might be wrong with her." Some people wouldn't let their kids around her in fear of what she may have. Walking into a doctor's office where I knew we had support and listening ears meant more to me than I can ever say.

With all that we were going through, and still trying to keep the Center's ministry going, and my husband's work, we needed to get away. We decided to go to Kingsport for a night. What makes this funny - and if you live around here you know this - Kingsport is not even 40 miles away from our home. We thought a day at Bays Mountain Park and

Our family on our one day vacation

a night at a nice hotel would be good for the family.

I felt we needed to get away from everyone we knew and just take time for each other - even if it was only for 24 hours.

We went to eat that night at Cheddar's and at three of the tables around us were friends we knew from our town. We just laughed and said God's reminding us of His army. We decided to just order

Hope enjoys breakfast in bed

in room service for breakfast. Hope was just smiling and seemed so happy. I took the cutest picture that made it look like she had a breakfast in bed.

After our brief respite, we returned to the now normal routine of work, doctor's appointments, tests and therapy sessions.

We have gone through so many tests. One test was an EEG at a local neurologist office. They had to place sticky glue wires all over Hope's head. I had to get her to sleep for the test to be completed without holding her. My friend Jodi Buckles was with me to help. Once they finally got all the wires on her head she would move around. I had my iPod with the songs that would help her go to sleep. One song that had been her lullaby from day one that I would sing to her is "What Love Is This" by Kari Jobe. All of her music would calm Hope, but it seemed that this particular song was her favorite. There we were, in the doctor's office exam room, and there I was, leaning over her trying to sing softly with music to get her to sleep. It was so hard not to just break down in tears knowing she was going through this. Jodi would look away when tears would come to help me be strong. Finally I was able to get her to sleep for the test to begin. The nurse was sitting behind me at the computer reading things and making notes on whatever the brain waves were doing. My heart was racing and I

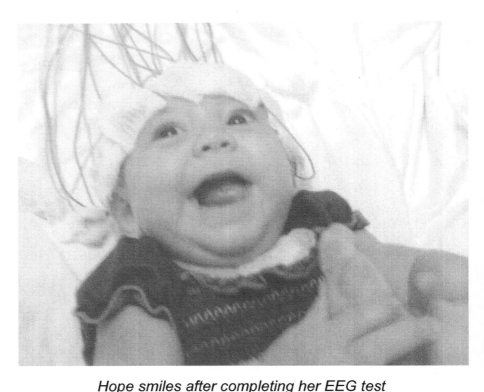
Hope smiles after completing her EEG test

was praying she would stay asleep. The test took about 40 minutes. Hope slept through it all, and then woke up and looked at me with a huge smile on her face. Of course I had huge tears running down my face.

We then went back to a room for the doctor to come talk to us. I shared with him my concerns. Hope would turn her hands and feet in a circle motion, especially when she was sitting with her legs out straight. Her feet would turn blue at times. That day we were told the EEG was normal but when we returned for a follow up appointment I was given a report saying her EEG was abnormal. The report said "localized slowing of the left Centrotemporal suggests an underlying focal encephalopathy, increased muscle tone in her legs." The doctor wanted her to continue physical therapy to help with the problem of persistent hypertonicity bilaterally - which is a technical way of saying she has increased tension of the muscles in both legs and the muscle tone in her legs is abnormally rigid which hampers her movement ability. The doctor called her condition "Transient Neuromotor Dysfunction." I left knowing something was noted that was wrong, but no clue what it meant or how to help my child overcome it.

We then made her an appointment with a neurologist in Knoxville, Tennessee. It took a few months to get Hope in to see this specialist. It always seems so hard to wait, but again God has helped me by reminding me "Be Still And Know

That I Am God". When we went to the first appointment at the Knoxville office the specialist spent a lot of time with Hope. My dear friend Tina Byrd went with me for this appointment. The doctor heard the history on Hope and I explained there wasn't much medical documentation to give him at this time. He checked her over and said he noticed a increased tone on one side. His assessment was Hemiplegic cerebral palsy and he wanted to order an MRI. On the way home I remember wondering if she will walk and play like other children. Even though I knew I needed to give this situation over to God, I still was hanging on to the worry. We asked others to pray for God to touch Hope and her situation. We waited for the day to have the test done, praying for God to be with her. We had to be at the hospital very early for the test, so our whole family went down the night before. Hope had to be sedated for the MRI. They had to try a couple of times to get the IV needle in. We had to hold her down, and the look in her eyes broke my heart. She looked at me with a panic in her eyes.

Hope during a therapy session

I thought of how scary it had to be for her when she was born, going through pain and having no family members with her, only the nursing staff to care for her. The medication started going through her IV and her little body went limp. We had to leave her so they could do the test. It seemed like the longest hour of our lives. We had to wait a few days for the results, but the test came back normal. I was so thankful God had answered another prayer, but I was also confused on where to go next to get help for Hope. The Neurologist wrote a letter strongly supporting ongoing therapy from a feeding standpoint.

During this time Hope had been attending physical therapy, occupational therapy and had just started speech therapy in Bristol, Tennessee. At her age it was hard because we would have all three sessions back-to-back or with just a thirty minute break. Their last appointment was at 4pm and it was 45 minutes away from my work. Hope goes to work with me.

Hope sits on my desk while I work

We did this for six months - three appointments, or more, a week for therapy plus her Tennessee Early Intervention sessions. Her therapists were so sweet and helpful to Hope. I know a lot of her goals were met through their help. The scariest part of going over there to therapy was Hope would choke during the car ride, and because of her issues she would throw up. With her feeding issues, she could not clear the vomit from her mouth, which created a serious choking hazard. If she was not assisted in clearing her mouth she could die from aspiration. Many times while driving I would have to pull over on the side of the road to help clear her mouth so she would not suffocate. It was very scary because while driving it is not always safe to just pull over and I was always afraid I would not be quick enough.

I just felt I needed to find someone that could have a different approach in her feeding therapy, and I felt Hope would do better if we didn't have to travel so far for her appointments. My goal was to research other choices for therapy.

Hope still has some issues with eating even now. Part of the problem is she does not chew food properly. She was diagnosed with a feeding disorder called "oral dysphagia." Feeding disorders include problems gathering food and getting ready to suck, chew, or swallow it. Hope can get the food to her mouth but once it is in her mouth she gets choked and strangled. She has problems with all different textures of food. Part of the problem is that her body has not fully developed the sensation to swallow. This is a common occurrence with oral dysphagia. Foods which are pureed or have a baby-food type texture stick to her tongue and make her gag and she has not developed the proper skills to chew food. Anything given to her which does not gag her is swallowed whole, which is also a choking hazard. Liquids must have their consistency thickened somewhat because of her issues swallowing. If the liquids are not thickened it presents a risk of aspiration - which is when the food or drink enters the pathway to the lungs instead of the stomach. Aspiration is what happens when someone eating or drinking says it "went down the wrong pipe." Liquids also cause problems with her reflux if they are not properly thickened. The bulk of her nutritional needs are met through the use of formula, which must be thickened with rice to reach the right consistency, but we are looking at other ways to better meet her nutritional needs.

At first, our Occupational Therapist Dr. Christy Isbell thought the issues with food could be a sensory issue, but after seeing Hope for a while she realized it had to be something more. It was during this time frame working with Dr. Isbell in August 2014 that we learned Hope had been diagnosed with oral dysphagia while still in the NICU at Sacred Heart. The hospital paperwork shows the caregiver - which at that time would have been Irene - received care education on oral dysphagia, but Earl and I did not learn about this diagnosis until August 2014, after Hope had already been in our care for 19 months.

When I talked to Dr. Isbell after learning of this diagnosis she said after observing Hope she had reached the same conclusion. Dr. Isbell has been such a blessing to our family and we are lucky she has become a part of Hope's treatment plan. She is a pediatric occupational therapist with specialized training in both Sensory Integration and Neurodevelopmental Treatment. She is also a professor of Occupational Therapy and has written two books on child development and collaborated on four other book series.

Working with Dr. Isbell has been such a wonderful thing for our family. I feel like we are finally making progress as to finding out what is going on with Hope. We finally have a diagnosis and I feel like we finally have a plan of action.

Dr. Isbell put us in contact with Kimberly Dismukes, a speech language therapist. Kimberly has also been a blessing to our family. She has done such in-depth observations and testing on Hope and is helping us develop Hope's care plan. After evaluating Hope, Kimberly told us that Hope's feeding development is at the level of a 6-month-old infant. Basically, if a 6-month-old can't eat it, Hope can't either. We are so thankful for our therapist and the company TalkBack Pediatric Therapy.

The nursing home where Marie is living also has reached out and tried to assist us with Hope's needs. I was visiting the nursing home and, like always, the director came up to give me a hug. She has been so kind and helpful throughout our journey. Once I explained our new issue with Hope, she asked me to wait while she went to get the nursing home's Certified Dietary Manager. The dietary manager came out and started explaining all the different foods I could puree for Hope and also how to prepare the food my family eats in a way that Hope can eat it. She even took me into the kitchen and allowed a cook to show me how to prepare it. At the nursing home, they work with a lot of patients who also suffer from feeding issues like oral dysphagia, so they know a lot about preparing food for people with these conditions. I also met a speech therapist that works with their patients - many of whom have problems eating. She also gave me some ideas on helping Hope. As I was leaving the director said she was going to check and see if she could assist us in getting some more help in therapy and talking to a dietitian. I left there with nutrient-rich milk shakes to try for Hope, special straws and a menu. It is so amazing how God places just the right people in our path at just the right moment in life.

In the mean time while all of this was going on, in October 2013 my daughter Bethany married her high school sweetheart Dylan. I was planning their wedding during the fall of that year. When my daughter and I were shopping for her dress, I of course had Hope with me. We walked around as Bethany was picking out dresses to try on. I noticed people looking at us funny, but I didn't catch on to the reason why at first. It wasn't until Bethany was in the fitting room and I was sitting in the floor in front of the mirror talking to Hope that I realized everyone thought it was Bethany's baby and she

Hope sits in as flower girl while her sister walked down the aisle

was just getting married. It is amazing how much Hope and Bethany do look alike.

It was like everyone else was receiving help with their shopping but no one would say much to us. We decided we didn't want to stay any longer. As we left I said "Hope tell your sister to hurry so we can go eat." You should have seen their faces -

shocked, yet realizing they just lost out on a possible sale. It made us understand first hand what other young moms go through each day. I wondered how many of the girls I have helped have faced this attitude when they are out in public with their children. I pray we will always encourage them and not just stand back and judge.

The wedding was beautiful. I never thought I would have one daughter walking down the aisle and one being pulled in a wagon as the flower girl. God is so amazing and full of surprises.

The week after the wedding - on October 23, 2013 - we went and filed for the adoption of Hope. We were very excited about giving Hope a new life and helping her understand each day what a miracle she is.

Earl and I with Hope when we filed for adoption

"Let your light so shine before men, that they may see your good works, and glorify your Father which is in heaven." ~ Matthew 5:16

Chapter Nine
Choices - Both Bad and Good

Tragedy struck Irene's family again.

In January, 2013, Irene's son Aaron, Marie's brother, suffered a serious medical incident which sent him to the hospital. Aaron had just been released from jail in Florida. While he was in jail, Aaron had written letters to Irene talking about the things he would need when he was released. Irene had come to rely on my family to assist her with her problems and she came to me with the letters. I helped her out by researching shelters and service organizations in the area of Florida where Aaron was. These were agencies that could help him find food and clothing and would provide shelter for him if he found himself homeless. Irene took the information I collected and mailed it to Aaron.

He had been out of jail for about a week and was living in a shelter when he suffered some kind of unknown medical emergency. Aaron began having a severe seizure and was transported to a hospital for treatment. It was later determined he had suffered a very severe stroke that left him completely paralyzed. He could move his eyes to blink to respond to questions and he had his mental capacity, but he was essentially trapped inside his own body.

Aaron, like his sister Marie and other members of their family, had battled drug addiction for most of his life. Also like others in his family, Aaron had a criminal record. One of Aaron's drugs of choice was something called Bath Salts - which is a synthetic form of meth. Bath Salts became popular because when the drug was first introduced it was sold in convenience stores and markets and it was not illegal - though in many states it now is. Bath Salts provide the user with a high similar to the one experienced on meth, but it would not show up on the drug screens which were in use at the time the substance came on the market. Drug use has been shown to cause medical conditions such as seizures, heart problems, strokes and organ damage in people who frequently use drugs. As she had with Marie, Irene called to me to ask my help for her son. Irene was just not able to deal with the medical issues which surrounded her son's care. I once again found myself talking to nurses and doctors trying to find out information. I learned that the doctors were not able to determine what caused the medical condition that left Aaron paralyzed. I wondered to myself - knowing the choices he had made in his life, his battle with addiction, and the effect that drug use has on the body - if the choices he had made led to his medical issues.

I spoke with nurses caring for Aaron and I learned he was able to communicate with them by blinking his eyes in a pattern for yes and no when they asked him questions. I was able to speak with him on the phone and the nurses would tell me if he blinked yes or no to my questions. I asked him if he would like for Irene to call him to talk to him and the nurse said he blinked the answer "yes." I talked to Irene and told her about my conversation with Aaron and how he wanted to speak to her. Irene was unsure and nervous about talking to him. She asked me "What do I say to him?" I remember looking at her and saying "Just tell him you love him."

While working to help Irene with Aaron, I was once again shown that God works in mysterious ways. I was searching for a preacher or someone to visit Aaron and witness to him. I knew the situation was bad and I did not want an opportunity for salvation to pass him by. I did not know anyone in Florida who I could turn to and ask them to go witness to this young man. And, as has happened so many times in my life, God sent the person I needed into my life just when I needed them most. A local pastor from Kingsport named Dwight Marlow, and his wife Shelby, have been active in supporting our

Center and its programs. One day, Dwight walked into my office while I was going through phone listings for churches in that area of Florida - hoping to find someone who would help. I was hoping someone would go visit Aaron, check to see he was being cared for, and witness to him. I had not been able to find anyone who was willing to do this. Dwight heard me on the phone and said "Hey, I have a cousin in Florida."

While he was standing there in my office, Dwight called his cousin, a man named Roy Marlowe, and told him about me and the ministry work I do through the Center. I then spoke with Roy and we talked for hours. A peace came over me as he agreed to go see Aaron and witness to him. Roy is not only a good Christian man, he is a man who is not afraid to step out and share his faith. Roy then began visiting Aaron every week, driving more than two hours each way, even though Aaron was a complete stranger to him.

One day Roy called me with good news - Aaron had accepted Christ as his Savior and had given his life over to God. Roy said he had witnessed to Aaron and prayed with him. He said he asked Aaron if he wanted to be saved and Aaron blinked that yes he did. After Aaron accepted salvation, Roy continued to visit him, have Bible studies with him and share faith with him.

These two men began their relationship as strangers but became brothers in Christ. In the approximately six months that Aaron spent in nursing homes and hospitals after his stroke, Roy was the only visitor he ever had.

As Aaron's condition changed he was transferred to several different facilities. Wherever he was transferred to, Roy followed along and continued to visit with him. Aaron's health began to deteriorate and he was taken back to the hospital.

I again tried to encourage Irene to call or visit him. I remember one night I just sat her down and had a very frank discussion with her. I told her if she did not at least call her son before he died she would regret it. A short time later, Irene told me she had called and spoken to Aaron and she was glad she did.

Aaron passed away two days later, with Roy by his side reading the Bible to him. Roy later told me he was looking for a verse on healing but the verse he ended up being led to read talked about God's forgiveness and how it is absolute. Roy said when he finished reading, he looked over and Aaron was not breathing. His passing was so peaceful that Roy had not even noticed as he sat next to him.

Aaron had made many bad decisions in his life, choices dealing with his drug use and his criminal past. I find comfort in the fact that no matter what choices he made in the past, his final choice in this life led to his salvation and an eternal life.

"For my father and my mother have forsaken me, but the Lord will take me in."

~ Psalms 27:10

Chapter Ten
A New Home For Hope

In September of 2013, Earl and I started the process for our home study with Appalachian Family Outreach, an organization which handles home studies in our area for families seeking to adopt a child. Larry Rose is the director, and he has helped many families through the adoption process. We were given a large amount of paper work to fill out and had to gather information such as physicals, fingerprints, financials, references, and many other things. We had to complete a home inspection and other meetings with Larry Rose over a period of time. In the meantime we filed for the adoption of Hope a week after my oldest daughter's wedding in October.

We hired an attorney to represent us in the adoption and the court appointed an attorney - known as a guardian ad litem - for Hope and one for Marie. The guardian ad litem is an attorney who is selected to act on behalf of a person who cannot act on their own behalf, to make sure that the person's best interest is considered. Each of these attorneys met with Irene, our family and viewed all of the medical records for Marie. The attorney appointed to represent Marie visited the nursing home to see her and learn about her condition from the medical staff there. When the attorneys met with Irene she agreed to the adoption of Hope by our family and signed paperwork approving the adoption.

There were additional legal steps which had to be taken due to Hope's birth father being unknown. An advertisement had to be placed in the newspaper in the county in Florida where Hope was born. The ad had to run for four weeks, and then there was a

30 days waiting period after the last week to give time for anyone to respond to the ad and claim parental rights. No word was ever heard from anyone due to this ad.

In January 2014 we were awarded guardianship of Hope, which meant no one else could adopt her without our approval or recommendation. Our final adoption was March 14, 2014. This was an emotional day. I remember sitting before the judge and hearing him award us the adoption. It was joyful but yet bittersweet knowing Marie's heartbreaking story. We thanked God for being with Hope and working out all the details for her life.

Family members and friends joined us at the Covered Bridge Cafe in downtown Elizabethton for a celebration after our hearing with the judge. This was our first meal as a family with our new daughter. Hope's best friend Kylie Hope Carr - who is Kristie and Matt Carr's daughter - was there for the celebration and she and Hope played together.

Earl with best friends Hope and Kylie

"And we know that all things work together for good to those who love God, to those who are called according to His purpose." ~ Romans 8:28

Chapter Eleven
Hope Goes Full Circle

Our family began sharing Hope's story of survival against the odds with others from the very beginning. We want this to serve not only as a testament to the miracle God had performed, but as a way of giving hope to others. We feel like if we don't share the story then God doesn't get the glory.

In August 2014, my husband Earl and I, along with our daughters Bethany and Hope, traveled to Pensacola, FL, to do just that... to share the story.

Due to the facts I had uncovered, and having never visited this area before, I felt very on edge about staying overnight there. I kept thinking of all the drugs and crime I had learned about in my search to find out what had happened to Marie. Bethany was 33 weeks pregnant with our granddaughter at the time, so this added a little more concern to our trip.

I had been in contact with Sacred Heart Hospital since we became the custodial guardians of Hope. I had contacted them to find out more about Hope's health issues and to try to learn more about Marie's stay at the hospital. Together, the hospital staff and I orchestrated a reunion for Hope and all of the people who had been a part of her miracle birth.

The day before we left, I received a phone call from Jon Byrd, one of the board members from the TLC Community Center. He surprised me with the news that the board members had personally paid for a rental van for trip to Florida and it was ready for us to pick up. With tears once again running down my face, I was so thankful again for God meeting our needs. We have a PT Cruiser, but with all that is needed for a baby and more room needed

Hope and Bethany on our trip to Florida

for our pregnant daughter this was a prayer answered. While traveling I looked in the back seat, saw both of our girls and just laughed. I never would imagined we would be riding down the road on the way to Florida with our new little girl and our pregnant oldest daughter.

I remember pulling up to the parking area for the hospital and it felt so strange. Hope had spent so much time at this hospital and yet I had never been here. Knowing how she had spent months here in her birth mother's womb and then her time in the NICU unit without any support from her family breaks my heart not only for her but for her birth mother Marie as well.

When we walked into Sacred Heart Hospital, a Christian hospital, the first thing I saw impressed upon me that God has a plan for everything – a large cut-glass cross was displayed in a lighted case. I saw this cross and nearly cried.

The cross in the lobby at Sacred Heart Hospital

Just days before Hope came into our lives, Earl and I had been preparing to help lead a marriage retreat. As part of the retreat, each couple is given a cross to carry to signify their commitment. Before the crosses are presented to the couples, the retreat leaders carry the, crosses for a time and pray over them.

As soon as I walked into the hospital and saw that cross, it hit me; they had been carrying Hope's cross and praying over her.

Everyone – from the dispatchers, emergency medical personnel who responded to the scene when Marie overdosed and the emergency room staff who cared for her when she arrived, to the nurses who cared for Marie through her pregnancy, the doctors who delivered Hope and the NICU nurses who cared for Hope after her birth – was present at the reunion. I wanted to meet the people involved in their care and share the full story of the miracle they played a part in. They were part of a miracle, but they didn't know what a miracle it was because they didn't know the whole story.

The reunion was an emotional time for not only our family, but for the caregivers as well. Many of them told me they very rarely get updates or know the outcomes on people they have cared for. One dispatcher said that in 30 years she had never heard back from even one call until now. Many of the people we spoke with said they are a part of a patient's life for a brief time in a critical moment, but they never get to hear the outcome - did the person survive, are they recovering.

Some of the caregivers at the reunion told me they were amazed when they saw Hope, because they wondered if she could even survive the pregnancy. One nurse told me that even though she did not believe in abortion, she had felt the hospital, the doctors and the family had made the wrong choice in allowing the pregnancy to continue because she didn't think the baby had a chance. She said she never imagined that Hope would survive all of the things she and Marie were facing while Marie was pregnant. She told me after meeting Hope, she knew she had been wrong. She said 'I will never again question God.' What an amazing and powerful thing. Our little Hope, just by living, helped strengthen this woman's faith.

At the reunion, I told the story of Hope, from the circumstances of her miracle birth to how she has grown and developed. I told them about the many different medical opinions and diagnoses we had been given and the therapy we had been through. I also shared with them an update on Marie's condition as well as some of Marie's personal story -

Hope and I with some of the nurses who cared for her

including the problems Marie faced that led to her overdose. Many of the caregivers were equally amazed that Marie had lived.

As I stood there speaking to this large group of people I was watching Hope, who cannot sit still for a minute, wander around the room through all of the people. God laid a thought upon my heart. My daughter, my Hope, was alive because of God's will and the care and attention of the people that I was speaking to. I was looking at that crowd and I thought 'God really does send an army when needed.' That is how I saw them, as God's army of caregivers who helped Hope fight her battle.

Our family with Hope's Army

Our family presented plaques and letters of appreciation to all of those involved in the care of Marie and Hope to commemorate their involvement in this miracle. Letters were prepared to present from Congressman Phil Roe, State Representative Kent Williams, and Carter County Mayor Leon Humphrey. The Director of Carter County Tomorrow, Tom Anderson, bought and donated beautiful picture of our local Covered Bridge, which has been recognized as the most photographed historic landmark in Tennessee. We had the frame engraved saying "The Place Where Hope Grows".

The TLC Community Center made a plaque with Hope's picture on it along with verse Jeremiah 29:11 "For I know the plans I have for you, declares the Lord, plans for welfare and not for evil, to give you a future and hope."

Many of the people at the reunion thanked us repeatedly for visiting them to share this story. I was feeling so grateful for them and all they had done, but they felt grateful for us for taking the time to share this story. Our family felt the reunion was something that needed to happen to share Hope's story. This not only allowed us the opportunity to meet some of the people instrumental in bringing our daughter into the world and hear their stories about caring for her, but it allowed us to share with them the full story of our little miracle and how they had played a part in it.

I had never been in a hospital that was so beautiful. They had gardens with landscaped

Earl and I with Hope in the Children's Garden

waterfalls. The hospital even had chain restaurants and a pharmacy. God didn't just send Marie and Hope to a hospital, He provided the very best.

Leaving the hospital was also emotional. This time Hope was leaving full circle with a mom, a dad and her sister. We took Hope over the bridge in Florida

Hope leaves Sacred Heart Hospital for the second time

to the beach. We were so overjoyed to see Hope walking on the beach carrying her own cross. There are no words to express how blessed we feel as a family for God allowing us to be the parents of Hope and be used to help Marie and Aaron.

Leaving Florida we all felt a peace we hadn't had since our journey first started with Hope. Through research and investigation, we felt as if we now have a full understanding of all that went on. We thanked those that played a part in both their lives, and we could now share this story in full, with a new found peace from God.

Our family continues to pray for Hope's birth family as they come to terms with the tragedies they have suffered. We will always be grateful to Irene for choosing our family to raise Hope. We will also be eternally grateful for her decision to choose life, even when the doctor's thought no hope was possible.

Many people have asked my husband and I if we plan to be honest with Hope when she becomes old enough to understand the miraculous story of her birth and the history of her family that led her to this point. My answer in this has always been yes, because we believe the truth shall set you free. In hiding this information from her we feel it would rob her of knowing the miracle that she really is. Our family will support her as she learns the story of her birth and we look forward to hearing her one day share her own testimony... and won't that be a day to see.

Our family

"For I know the plans I have for you, declares the Lord, plans for welfare and not for evil, to give you a future and a hope." – Jeremiah 29:11

About the Author:

Angie Odom

My name is Angie Odom and I would like to share a part of my testimony with you. Through this book you have learned a good deal about my family, but I would like to now share with you the story of how I came to found the Abortion Alternatives and the TLC Community Center - which are a large part of the story told in this book. If I had never experienced the things in my life I am about to share with you I would never have created the Center and would not have met the child who has become my daughter. The story I am about to share with you is very personal, but I feel it is very important to share it so you may better understand my experiences and come to an understanding of how everything we go through in our lives prepares us for the work God has planned for us.

I grew up the daughter of a preacher. At a young age I lost my father to cancer and like so many who experience a tragic loss at a young age I went through a rebellious phase where I blamed God for my loss. I ended up joining the United States Navy where I met my first husband, Tracy Lee Crouch. It was during my time in the Navy that I renewed my relationship with God. It was this renewed relationship that gave me the strength I would need to face the ordeals that lay before me.

During my marriage to Tracy, God blessed me with my daughter Bethany. However, there were trials to endure along with the blessings. During my marriage I experienced domestic violence as I watched my spouse battle addiction. Four months into our marriage I got an emergency Red Cross alert. I was in the Philippines and he had already completed his service and had been discharged from the military. I was flown back to the United

States due to the fact that he had been involved in a car crash. Tracy was under the influence of drugs when he crashed his car. This was how I found out my husband had a substance abuse problem. The head injury Tracy sustained in this car crash changed his personality. That combined with his substance abuse is what led to the domestic violence issues.

From that point on living with Tracy was like having to constantly hold my breath, I never knew when he would lash out or why. We were married for almost five years. We had Bethany during the last year of our marriage. Prior to Bethany being born, I had two miscarriages as a result of the domestic violence. I finally found the strength and courage to leave my husband in order to save my life and the life of my daughter. Once I left, I realized that my battles were not over. I spoke to pastors and community service providers trying to find counseling and assistance as I now found myself a single mother. Because I worked, there were no assistance programs for which I qualified.

The pastors I spoke with offered little support because I was a divorced woman and single mother. But my faith in God carried me through and He provided for me.

God sent me a man named Earl Odom, who has been my partner in all things. Earl and I married in Oct. 1993 and he adopted my daughter Bethany. I went to college to continue my education and worked as the director of the Extended School Program at Elizabethton City Schools. While in college God, laid it on my heart to write a paper on abortion. In writing that paper He laid it on my heart to start a program to help provide an alternative to abortion to young women who find themselves in a crisis and feel they have no alternative.

Where God calls He also provides, and 14 years ago I founded Abortion Alternatives & Women's Center. We serve as a crisis pregnancy center for unmarried and married clients. We offer them support and services from the time pregnancy is confirmed through the child's first year of life We assist them in obtaining not only items needed for the child - such as food, diapers, clothing, car seats and baby beds. We also provide parenting classes and referrals for counseling for substance abuse or domestic violence as well as referrals to other assistance programs, such as public housing. During our 14 years, our Center has seen many needs within the community and God has continued to bless us by assisting us in growing to meet those needs.

In 2013 we founded the TLC Community Center which, in addition to Abortion Alternatives & Women's Center, includes the following programs: the Summer Food Program which provides meals to children during the summer months when school is not in session; the Guard Your Heart abstinence program which is taught in all of the Carter County High Schools; Food For the Multitude which works with area churches to provide meals to the community on weekends; a community soup kitchen; and Little Feet Children's Ministry, which is geared toward helping the special needs children of our community. Our Center also provides space to TalkBack Therapy - which provides physical, occupational and speech therapy to children - to better serve our clients since many of them faced long drives in order to obtain these needed therapies for their children. The TLC Community Center also features other programs as well and we look forward in the future to expanding the programs we offer as we strive to continue meeting the needs of our community. In the future we hope to have office space to allow professional counselors in the areas of substance abuse and domestic violence to come in to the Center and meet with our clients and others in the community who have a need of their services. These services are desperately needed in our community and are not readily available. Believe me, I know. I see it every day working with the clients of our Center.

I have forgiven Tracy for what I experienced at his hands during our marriage. I named the new part of the center The TLC Community Center, not to honor what Tracy Lee Crouch did, but to represent true healing and forgiveness because had it not been for what I experienced in my marriage to him I would not have went down this path in my life. I would not have come to understand that these are true needs in our community that are not being met.

Our daughter Bethany wanted to meet her birth father in order to learn his story not just from my experience but from his own words. She met him twice. The third time she ever saw him was in 2009 at his funeral. Now Earl and I have started on a new journey in life which God has sent us on. We adopted an infant who was born to a client of our Center. This book is the story of our daughter Hope's birth and what a miracle it truly was. As we are presented with new challenges we continue to pray that God gives us the strength and means to face them and to help us provide assistance to the community.

About the co-Author:

Abby Morris-Frye

My name is Abby Morris-Frye. I am a journalist with the newspaper in my hometown, The Elizabethton Star. I have been working as a volunteer with Angie Odom at Abortion Alternatives and the TLC Community Center since 2009, but I knew her through my work at the newspaper before I became a volunteer. I have been married to my husband Stephen Frye for 10 years, and he has been such a blessing to my life. I am the daughter of Brady and Debbie Morris, and my father also volunteers at the Center.

I was volunteering at the Center on that cold February morning when Hope first came into our lives. I remember how tiny she was and being astonished at the miracle God had performed with her birth. I had also known Hope's mother Marie.

As a child I always dreamed of being a writer and of one day writing my own book. Over the years I kept the love of writing and went on to major in journalism at East Tennessee State University. I still kept the dream of one day writing a book in my heart, but I never suspected that God would lay before me such a wonderful story for me to help tell in my first book. This precious child, whose story you are holding in your hands, has already touched the lives of so many people in her short life - and that includes me.

I am so glad God chose me to help share this wonderful story of a miracle and to help share Hope with others.

About the Miracle

Hope

My name is Hope. I've had to fight hard to overcome some things since I was born but God has been holding my hand the whole way.

I wake up each morning with a smile on my face thanking

God for the day and my family. I love books! Baby Bear, Baby Bear is my favorite but I have about nine that I love for daddy to read. I also like to play with the dogs at my house and my Mamaw's.

My dad and I go in the backyard everyday and feed corn to the deer and pick tomatoes and cucumbers from our little garden. I like to climb on anything I can. I love my big sissy and get to spend time with her everyday. I'm now an aunt and can't wait to show Sophia all the things I've learned to do. My mom and I go everywhere together. I help her at work everyday. I love to go to lunch at Dino's in town. Dave and Red run the place, and they let me ring the bell for the orders every time I go and I get a lollipop. I know all my animal sounds, so when I go feed the ducks I quack at them the whole time. I love Kari Jobe songs and my favorite show is Baby Einstein Old McDonald.

I'm thankful for what God has done in my life and can't wait to learn how to do things for Him.